PASS THE
B1 SPEAKING AND
LISTENING ENGLISH TEST
FOR BRITISH CITIZENSHIP
AND SETTLEMENT
(OR INDEFINITE LEAVE
TO REMAIN)

D1428528

With Practice Questions and Answers

ISBN: 978-1-910662-26-7

First Published 2016
Revised in 2018
Copyright © 2018

CONTENTS

Chapter 1

Introduction to the test

The English language speaking and listening test is an important part of the process if you want to become a permanent resident or a naturalised British citizen. You must pass this test and supply the results as proof of your English language ability in your application. This test is done separately from the Life in the UK test but the results count towards the final assessment. You will need to send the details of your language test result together with the confirmation of the results from your Life in the UK test to the Home Office as part of your application.

There are thousands and thousands of people who take the speaking and listening test for visas every year, but not everyone who takes the test passes. With an attempt costing around £150 a time, this can be very expensive for people who fail and who need to take the exam again. However, if you understand what you need to do, prepare and practise, then you can be confident that you will pass the first time. This book will help you to prepare for the test.

There are two speaking and listening tests that are accepted by the UK Home office for these visas. They are the IELTS Life Skills and the Trinity GESE Grade 5 exam, and you can choose which test to take. Although they differ in the format and the length, both tests check that the candidate or 'test taker' shows enough English to match the descriptions in the Common European Framework Reference for that level also known as 'CEFR'.

If you are already living in the UK and you want to settle, or if you want to become a British citizen, you need to take the test at CEFR B1 level. Both IELTS SELT Consortium and Trinity College London are approved to offer this test by the UK Border Agency. You only need to take a test for your spoken English and listening skills for these visas, so you do not need to worry about your reading and writing ability in English being tested.

But make sure that you actually need to take the English language exam in the first place as you may find that you do not have to take a test at all. For example, if you are from a majority English speaking country or if you have a degree that was taught in English you do not have to take the test.

About this book

This book will guide you in easy to understand and everyday language on how to pass the speaking and listening English language tests for a visa for indefinite leave to remain known as 'settlement' or citizenship.

The first part of the book gives some information on the difference between the two tests offered by the two providers, which may help you to decide which one to take. You will then find a description about what you will need to do for each provider to apply for British Citizenship or settlement. The book offers advice on how to prepare for the tests and how to do well on the day. At the end you will find some practice questions and answers with some practical tips on how to answer the questions well in the exam.

The information in the book is correct at the time of writing.

Who is the book for?

You may be planning to take one of the tests yourself and be unsure about which one to choose, or you may want to know more so you can feel confident about doing well in the interview. Perhaps you want to help a friend, partner or family member to understand and prepare for the test.

This book is for people who have busy lives and who want a general overview of the exam and advice on how to do well. You will find important information about the tests with tips so that you will pass and go on to use your results in your visa application.

How can I use this book?

All the information in this book will help you in the language tests so you may want to read through it chapter by chapter. Or, you might like to choose sections of the book that are most useful to you or the person who you are helping.

It's a good idea to make notes in the margin and use a highlighter pen to mark sentences or sections that are you think are particularly important.

Why do I have to take an English language test?

In 2010 the UK government decided that it was better for society if migrants could speak English as this would promote integration into British society, and also reduce the tax cost for UK residents. Since that date, there have been many changes to the laws and decisions on who needs to take the test. This book contains the information and requirements from January 2016.

You need to show that you can speak English to the level decided by the UK government to get the type of visa you are applying for, and your ability is tested in a face-to-face interview.

What does the test prove?

The test checks that your English level matches the descriptions of the B1 CEFR in the Common European Framework. This is the level that has been decided that people need to reach to be given citizenship or settlement. When you have passed this test then the authorities will accept that you are able to use and understand language of this level and you will have satisfied this part of the visa application process.

How will my level of English judged?

You may be asking yourself: *'What will the examiner use to check how well I speak English?'*

If you are applying for a visa for indefinite leave to remain, also known as 'settlement', or applying for British citizenship, also known as 'naturalisation', then you will be an 'Independent User' and will need to take a test at the CEFR B1 level. The CEFR, which stands for 'The Common European Framework of Reference for languages, is an international guide by the Council of Europe. It is used to describe the language ability of learners and is used by the examiners to judge your English level. This standard is recognised by governments, universities and employers as a clear and objective way to rate a learner's skills in different languages. It is used all over the world.

There are six levels given to language learners in this guide. The first level is A1, which is the level for very basic learners. The levels then move on to A2, B1, B2, C1, and finally the exam for very advanced learners which is the C2 level.

Generally, the tests at each level measure your ability in speaking, listening, reading and writing. But remember, you will only need to prove your speaking and listening skills for the visa for settlement or citizenship. Also, you can see that the B1 test is quite a long way before the C2 level for Advanced Users, and just above the A2 test which is for Basic Users. You can see this in the table below. This should help you to understand that the B1 level isn't too difficult and you aren't expected to speak at a very high level.

C1 to C2 – Advanced Users

B1 to B2 – Independent Users

A1 to A2 – Basic Users

As we saw before, if you take the B1 test then you are called an 'Independent User'. Here is a list of what an Independent User can do according to the CEFR:

- You can understand the key points of conversation on familiar topics that you meet regularly at work, school or in your free time.

- You can deal with typical situations while travelling.

- You can say simple connected sentences on familiar topics or topics that you are personally interested in.

- You can describe experiences and events, your hopes and ambitions for the future, explain and give reasons for your plans and opinions.

You will find advice and tips later in the book on how to show that you can do this.

What will I have to do in the B1 test?

The format of the speaking and listening test is different for the IELTS Life Skills test and the Trinity GESE test. Results from both tests are accepted by the UK government as proof of your ability to speak English to the required level, the B1 CEFR level.

It is important that you show that you are able to use and understand the language given in the specifications at the B1 level. The examiner will listen carefully to what you say and will probably match your language against a checklist they have in front of them to see how closely similar it is. This checklist is based on the language required for the level you are taking and so it is this that you need to demonstrate.

So, basically, to do well you have to make sure that you cover what is in the requirements and use the language that the examiner is looking for! The examiner will also be looking at how clearly you speak, how well you interact, how well you can understand and how well you can express yourself.

What is the difference between the two tests?

There are different tasks to be completed in the Trinity GESE Grade 5 Test and in the IELTS Life Skills test. The number of tasks you have to do in each test differs too. However, both tests are based on the descriptions of an Independent User in the CEFR and it is this that you need to match. You will learn more about the tasks in each test later in the book.

You can decide which test to take and your decision may depend on the dates and the places the test is available. It's a good idea to know as much as you can about the test before you enter the exam room and meet the examiner.

Chapter 2

What is the examiner looking for?

There is a specific description for the English language skills of a B1 Independent User that you need to show you can match in the interview. You will have to show that you have a certain level in different areas. These areas are fluency, how well you interact in English, pronunciation, language accuracy and your range of vocabulary.

It is important to know that the examiner does not expect your language level to be of a very high level or at a level similar to a person who was born and has lived in the UK all their life. You will not be expected for example, to talk about difficult abstract ideas and to speak for a long time. And, the examiner will not be looking to see if you can speak very precisely. But you will be expected to talk quite simply about familiar things and situations you often meet such as when you travel.

You will be expected to show that you can interact with others in English, talk with some fluency, speak quite accurately, show a range of vocabulary, listen and understand others, and speak clearly enough for people to understand what you say. Below you will find more information on these areas that the examiner will be looking for. Later in the book you will find some advice on how you can do well in these different areas.

How well you interact

You may be alone with the examiner or there may be another test taker with you, depending on the test you decide to take. In both tests, the examiner will be looking to see if you can understand what is being said and can get information. You can show this by interacting with the others in the room and doing things such as making comments, agreeing, interrupting, asking people to repeat or explain, and asking questions.

If you don't say very much and just answer any questions directed to you with one or two words, then you will probably not do very well in this area. And if you are in the interview room with another test taker, there is no hiding! The examiner will be judging the performance of both of you so you will need to make an effort and speak. You will not be judged on your opinions or as a person but just on what you do and the English you can show in the test itself. This is not a time to be shy and say very little!

Talking with fluency

How well you talk and express facts, opinions and your feelings will be judged. Can you talk quite comfortably or do you find it difficult to put the words together to say sentences? You are expected to talk with little problem. Remember, as an Independent User you do not have to use complicated sentences and difficult long words. If you try to use words and phrases you are more comfortable with in the interview, then this means you will probably speak without stopping and more fluently.

If you find that you often stop, you can't find anything to say or you find it very difficult to find the words to say what you want, then you will probably not do well in this area.

However, at this B1 level it is perfectly OK to pause for a moment or two to think now and again. Speaking fluently does not mean you have to speak fast and without a break. At this level speaking fluently means you can talk slowly and clearly without showing much difficulty. And of course if you find it difficult to say what you want to then it's OK to stop and just try to say it a different way.

How accurate are you?

You need to show that you have a good control of your spoken English. This does not mean that are expected to speak perfectly and that you cannot make any mistakes at all. At this level it is fine to make a few mistakes. And remember the examiner is looking for different things and not just how precisely you can speak.

You will probably be talking about topics that you should be quite familiar with, such as your hobbies and travel, and you will be talking about things that you talk about frequently in everyday life too. This means that you will probably not have to think too long and hard about what to say and can concentrate on speaking as correctly as you can with few mistakes.

Your range of words

You will need to show that you are confident in using a variety of words when talking about subjects that you are familiar with or meet frequently. If the subject is completely new to you then you might have problems finding the right words, but this is OK at this level. The examiner will allow for this. As you will be talking about subjects that you are familiar with, you can try to include a good variety of words to show how much you know.

Remember that if you don't understand a word or an expression you can ask the examiner what it means. Of course if you ask too many times the conversation will not go very well and you may not make a good impression, but asking for some help could show that you can interact well and are active in trying to understand. It's better to ask so you understand than to continue without understanding what the examiner means. If you do then the result could be confusing for both of you and for the others in the room!

On a final note here, try to be careful not to use words that are slang or too informal. It wouldn't be appropriate for example to greet the examiner by saying 'Hello mate.' You should use a little more formal language such as 'Good morning.' Of course this doesn't mean that you have to use language that is unnatural for you but just try to be polite and not too familiar.

Can you listen and understand?

You will need to show that you can listen and understand subjects that you are familiar with and that are organised in a way that is simple to follow. The examiner (and the other test taker if you are doing a test where there are two test takers in the room) will ask you some questions. You will need to respond well and reasonably quickly to their questions to do very well in the test.

You may have to listen to some recordings and complete an exercise on what you have heard. You will only have to do this for one of the tests, the IELTS Life Skills test. This will probably include listening to a talk or an announcement that is quite direct and easy to follow, or some directions or instructions on how to do something or work a simple piece of equipment.

How well can people understand you?

No doubt you will speak English with the accent of your own country. This is not a problem at all and there is no reason to worry about this as the examiner will not look at how strong your accent is. The guidelines state that others should be able to clearly understand you and a foreign accent does not usually have any effect on this. However, you must speak as clearly as possible. You can judge if your accent is difficult to understand by thinking how often people do not understand you when you talk in English. Do people ask you to repeat often? Do they say *'Sorry? I didn't understand what you said?'* If this happens a lot to you then you need to work on improving how clearly you speak.

Do you often mispronounce words? Although you are not expected to pronounce every word perfectly, if you pronounce many words badly it may be difficult to follow what you say.

Chapter 3

*Comparing the two
B1 tests*

This section will give you information about the two different tests and tell you what you have to do during the tests. You can take either the IELTS B1 Life Skills or the Trinity GESE Grade 5 test. Both exams reflect typical situations you experience when you communicate with others in an English speaking country.

Both tests can be used in your application for indefinite leave to remain (settlement) or citizenship. And for both tests, the results last for two years. If you fail, then there is no limit to how many times you can retake the test so you can just try again.

Make sure the centre where you take your test is called a *SELT centre.* This stands for Secure English Language Test. Only results from tests taken at these centres will be accepted for your visa application.

Here is a quick overview of the two exams.

	Trinity GESE Grade 5	**IELTS B1 Life Skills**
Length	10 minutes	22 minutes
Test taken alone	✓	
Number of parts in test	2	3
Topic presentation	✓	
Listening task		✓

In both exams you will talk about subjects that allow you to show you can manage the language of the CEFR B1. As we saw before, these are usually topics that you are familiar with and meet every day. Possible subjects that you may meet in the exam are as follows:

• family and friends

• hobbies

• shopping and buying things

- your job and work in general

- your health

- free time and entertainment

- education/training

- transport and travel

- housing

- things that have happened to you and events/experiences

The IELTS Life Skills Test.

This section will give you some information about this test and what you have to do in the interview.

You can take this exam in many parts of the world. The result is either pass or fail. If you receive a fail, then you cannot use the test result in your application for a visa.

This test lasts a total of 22 minutes. However, you will not be expected to talk all that time as you will go into the interview room with another test taker and share the time given. You may ask why you have to be with another test taker. The reason given is that the test will judge your skills at communicating with another person and at having a discussion. The examiner has the job of judging the language skills of both of you at the same time.

The idea of being with another test taker may be a little frightening for you. You may ask yourself if the other test taker's performance will have an effect on you and if it will affect the way the examiner judges your English ability. You don't have to worry about this. The examiner will be trained and experienced in this and will judge each test taker separately from the other test taker.

The other test taker is in same situation as you so very probably they will be nervous too. Smile and be friendly to the other person. If they feel comfortable, then you may feel less nervous too and the interaction between you may go better.

If you do not understand what the other person says, make sure you ask them to repeat what they said. It's important to continue to speak if you can, and not allow your performance to be influenced by how well or badly you feel the other person is doing.

This test is broadly divided into just two sections but there are five different tasks that you will have to do and be ready for:

In the first part:

• ask and answer personal questions (up to 3 minutes)

• give a short talk and ask questions (up to 7 minutes)

In the second part:

• listen to two different recordings and answer some questions (up to 5 minutes)

• plan an activity (up to 3 minutes)

• ask and answer questions about a specific topic (up to 4 minutes)

You will find more about what happens in each task below:

Personal questions

You will go into the exam room together with the other test taker. In this part you will have to **answer and ask some simple questions** so the examiner can get to know you and the other person.

At first the examiner will introduce themselves to you and ask each of you some simple questions such as: *'What's your name?'*

'What's your nationality?' or *'How long have you been here?'* The examiner will then tell you to ask the other test taker some questions. You will be told the subject to ask the questions about. For example, you may be told to ask questions about the town or city the other person is from. The examiner may also ask you some questions so be ready to answer the examiner's questions too!

A short talk

You will then have to **give a short talk** of about one minute and a half. The examiner will tell you what you have to talk about. This might be something like: *'You are going to talk about a place that you visited that you enjoyed a lot.'*

You will be given one minute to write some notes to help you in your talk and there will be a pen and some paper for you on the desk. Try not to write down full sentences as this will slow you down and might mean you just read them out. You might like to use a mind map to get down your ideas quickly instead of writing a list of points. Using a mind map will help you to look down quickly at your notes and see your points immediately instead of reading them. You will then be able to speak more clearly without pausing.

Here is an example of a mind map that you could make in preparation for a talk on a place that you visited that you enjoyed a lot.

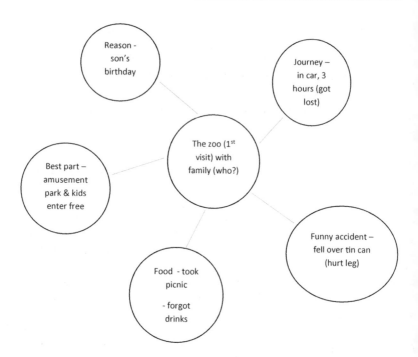

The other test taker will be told to ask you some questions about your talk, so be ready to answer their questions.

The other test taker will also have to give a talk. When the other test taker has finished talking about the subject they have been given, you will have to ask them three questions about what they said. So it's very important to listen carefully to the other candidate when they talk! Your questions can be simple such as: *'What did you eat when you stayed in the hotel?'*, *'Did you enjoy staying in the hotel?'* and *'How long did you stay in this hotel?'*

In the next part of the test the examiner will be assessing your speaking skills together with your listening skills.

Listening task

You will then have to **listen to two recordings** and **answer a question** on what you hear in one of the recordings. You will be offered a pen and paper and it's a good idea to write down some words or notes to help you remember. The notes are just for you so don't worry about your writing during this test as the examiner will not look at this. The subject on the recording will be one that you are familiar with, such as transport. The recordings may be the typical kind of announcements you hear at the airport or at a train station.

The examiner will then ask you to listen and then note down **what each talk is about**. You will be asked to say what just one of the recordings is about. The examiner will say for example: *'What type of transport is the second recording about? A plane, a train or a car?'* You will not know if the examiner will ask you a question about the first or the second recording, so it's important to listen and make notes carefully about both recordings.

You will then have to listen to the two recordings again and answer a question about some **specific information** you hear. Before the recordings are played again the examiner will tell exactly what you have to listen for. For example you may hear *'Candidate A: In the second recording, what time will the train arrive? And why is there a delay?'* The information that you will have to listen for will be different to the information that the other test taker will have to listen for, so listen carefully to the examiner's questions!

The examiner will give you clear instructions on what you have to do before each listening task. If you don't understand what you have to do, or if you are unclear, then just ask.

Planning together

You will then have to **plan and discuss something together** with the other test taker. The examiner will give you some information on a piece of paper or booklet to look at and will read out the information to you too. You will need to use this information in your discussion. A typical situation might be that you have to plan where to take a visitor who is coming to your city. You may be given information about what you could possibly do and what transport you could use such as *go shopping, visit museums, go sightseeing*, and the transport you could use: *bus, tram, bicycle.* You will have to discuss this using the information and make a decision with the other test taker. The examiner will listen carefully to how well you communicate and exchange ideas in English.

Finding out information from the other test taker.

Finally, the examiner will ask you to talk to the other test taker and **ask some questions to find out some information about a given topic**. You will be given a topic such as free-time activities and the topic will probably be closely related to what you discussed in the task before. As an example, the examiner could ask you to find out what hobbies the other test taker had when they were a child and that they have now.

You can see that you will have to interact with the other test taker who will be in the same room with you. You may ask yourself what will happen if you feel shy or nervous and don't ask the other test taker any questions. Perhaps even both you *and* the other test taker could feel this way! If this does happen, then the examiner will step in and ask some questions to you both to help get the conversation going.

Remember, it is your English the examiner is judging and so they want you to be able to speak as much as possible so they can assess your language level. The examiner will help you to show your English level. However, you will probably do better and make a better impression if you can speak well and confidently without the examiner stepping in too often. There are examples of the type of language at B1 level that you should aim to use later in the book in the section on Language Practice.

Trinity GESE Grade 5 test

Below you will find some information about Trinity College's GESE Grade 5 test and what you will have to do in the interview.

You can only take this exam at one of the approved centres in the UK. This test is not offered in any other countries. You will receive your result on the day immediately after the test but should wait for around 7 days to receive the formal confirmation. If you receive a fail then you cannot use the test result in your application for a visa.

This test lasts a total of 10 minutes. This test is different from the IELTS Life Skills test as there will just be you and the examiner in the interview room. The examiner will talk to you and will judge your language skills against the B1 criteria. However, in this test the examiner will be specifically checking to see if you can do the following in English in particular:

- talk about future plans and what will happen
- say what you prefer
- talk about recent events and experiences
- give reasons
- say how long events and experiences lasted
- say how much and how many

Try to use language that covers these points in your topic and conversation as much as you can. There are examples of what language to use in the section on Language Practice later in the book.

The thought of being interviewed by someone for ten minutes as part of your visa application may make you feel nervous and this is very natural. However, to get a pass you only to need to give a short talk about a topic that you choose, respond to questions as clearly and as well as you can and ask a few questions. The examiner will want you to do as well as you can and so will very probably be pleasant and helpful to you.

This test has two parts: a topic of your choice and a conversation about two different subjects. You will find more about each part and what you will have to do below.

The topic

In the first task you will have to talk about a topic that you are interested in for up to 5 minutes. You should prepare this before you go into the interview room. Before you go into the room, you will be given a mind map to complete with a few words in each box to help you to talk about your topic. Ideally you should download the empty mind map from the Trinity website and spend time preparing this before you go along to the exam on the day. The examiner will look at the different boxes and ask you questions about the ideas you've written in each box. As the idea is that you have a discussion about your topic, you are expected to ask the examiner some questions too.

So what should you talk about in your topic? You will probably do better if you talk about something that you are interested in or that is personal to you. The examiner will not be testing your knowledge so you are not expected to be an expert in the topic you choose! Choosing something that you are interested in will help you to speak confidently and well.

Here is a list of subjects that could help you to decide on your topic.

My best holiday ever   Summer plans

Films I enjoy   The football team I support

My job   Places I visited in the UK

My life in the UK

My favourite film

Playing the piano

My family back home

My family in the UK

Sports that I enjoy

My career so far

My favourite writer

My country

A true friend

Music in my life

Cooking at home

My home town

My favourite football team

A book that I liked

My children

My car

The day I got married

On your mind map you need to write your ideas in a few words in each of the five boxes. You may not be sure what to include on your mind map so here is an example:

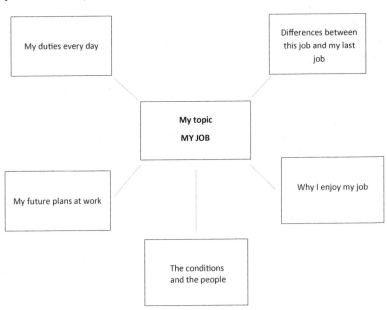

You can see above that you write the title of your topic in the middle box and the points in the boxes around the title that will help you to talk about the topic in depth. The examiner will probably choose one of the boxes in turn and ask you questions.

You will have up to five minutes to talk about the different points in your mind map but don't worry if you don't talk about all items in the boxes. The examiner may just choose four because of time limits.

You are not expected to talk without stopping and the examiner will also ask you some questions about each of your points. Remember that the examiner will also be looking at how well you interact with them and understand their questions. So allow time in your planning for questions and also pause now and again to let them ask a question. You may not do well if you try to memorise your whole talk, speak too quickly about all your points and do not give space for any interaction. The examiner will always be looking at how well you interact with them and how well you understand what is being said and checking that what you say is appropriate.

Remember that you need to ask questions to the examiner too. For example: *'And what about you?'* *'What do you like about your job?'*

The conversation

In the second task you will have a conversation with the examiner about two different subjects. This part lasts up to five minutes.

The subjects are chosen by the examiner from a short list of topics and you will know what these subjects are in advance. In 2016 the subjects for conversation are festivals, entertainment, recent experiences, special occasions, music and transport. You will need to talk with the examiner about two of these for around 2 to 3 minutes for each subject.

In this conversation part of the test you should also ask the examiner some questions about the subject you are talking about. You may find the examiner has asked you about the subject of special occasions for example so you could ask a question such as: *'What was the last thing you celebrated?'* You may feel shy or nervous or you may even find this difficult to do, but it's important you ask a few questions during this part of the test as this is a requirement of the exam.

You may even find it helpful to go into the interview room with a few questions ready to ask about the different subjects. Remember, the examiner wants to check your language ability against the guidelines they have and so they want to see if you can ask questions too! For some examples of questions at B1 level go to the chapter on Language Practice.

Chapter 4

*How can I do well
in the test?*

In this section you will find some practical advice on how to improve your ability to speak without difficulty, your grammar, your range of words, pronunciation, and listening skills.

The more you practise before the interview, the more prepared you will be and then the more confident you will feel. If you do not speak regularly in English then make an effort to go out and practise by speaking to people. One way to do this is to go into shops and ask for information for example. Ask family members at home who speak English well to speak to you only in English and not in your native language. Instead of watching television channels in your own language, choose to watch programmes in English, even if it's just for a short time each day.

If you have lived and worked in an English speaking country for many years, then you are very probably communicating at B1 level already. However, knowing about what is expected of you in the exam will help you to do very well with a minimal effort.

Below is some advice on how to improve the areas the examiner will be checking for.

Your range of words

You will need to talk about topics from your everyday life and use a range of words to do this well. Earlier in the book we saw that the main topics for discussion in the B1 exam are:

- your hobbies

- your family and friends

- shopping and buying things

- your job and work in general

- your health

- free time and entertainment

- transport and travel

- your home and housing

You may at times make some mistakes with the words you use and this is perfectly fine in the interview. At B1 level the examiner will allow for a few mistakes. However, if you make many mistakes then of course you will not give a very good impression to the examiner. So try your best to use the words in their correct form.

The examiner will be looking to see if you can use a variety of words to talk about the everyday topics that will come up in the test. This does not mean that you have to use a very wide range of words or that the words you use will have to be very complicated. Remember, this is an elementary exam so the examiner will not expect a very high level of vocabulary from you. However, the better the variety and range of words you use, the more you will impress the examiner.

So how can you improve your range of words? One way to do this is to make mind maps for each subject and add words to each map. Look at the mind map for the topic of the cinema below for example:

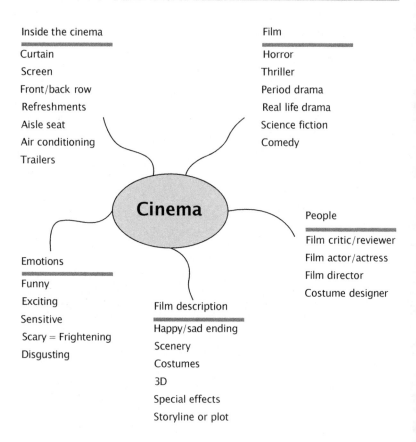

Inside the cinema

Curtain
Screen
Front/back row
Refreshments
Aisle seat
Air conditioning
Trailers

Film

Horror
Thriller
Period drama
Real life drama
Science fiction
Comedy

Cinema

People

Film critic/reviewer
Film actor/actress
Film director
Costume designer

Emotions

Funny
Exciting
Sensitive
Scary = Frightening
Disgusting

Film description

Happy/sad ending
Scenery
Costumes
3D
Special effects
Storyline or plot

You could write in opposite meanings of the words or translations to help you as in the map above.

Look back at the list of topics that may come up during the exam. You will find it helpful to draw some mind maps such as this for the topics that you are not very familiar with. This will help you to expand your word range and bring a lot of words that are connected to the topic to your mind.

You will find that just the process of doing a mind map will help you to learn the words and see how they are connected to the topic. A quick look now and again at the map will help you memorise the words, and then you will be able to use them in your daily life and, importantly, be able to use them with little effort in the exam.

If the examiner asks you a question about one of these topics then this is the opportunity to include some of the words in your answer.

Another way to improve your range of words is to read as much as you can. This does not mean you have to read long difficult books. You can easily make your range of words wider by reading short articles in newspapers or on the internet. If you have a hard copy, then underline some of the words you think are useful to you in your everyday life.

The free newspapers you find when you travel in some cities are an excellent source of vocabulary for common everyday topics. You can also buy, or find in your local library, easy reading books called 'readers' that are especially for learners of another language and are often short versions of original well known books.

Remember that in the exam you need to be active in showing your knowledge of words and your skills in communicating with them in English. Try to do this as naturally as you can, but at the same time make an effort to use as many of the words on the topic that you know.

If you find that you want to say something but cannot think of the word you want to use, then think of another way to say it. You could even say *'I'm sorry I can't think of the word,* and *what I mean is...'* This will show you have good communication skills as you are showing that you can explain yourself in difficult situations.

Your pronunciation

The examiner will be checking that you can speak in English in a way that people can understand you, and ideally, the first time you say something. This does not mean that you should not speak with a foreign accent of course. The examiner will allow for accents from different countries and even expect this, especially if they find that you have not lived in an English speaking country for a long time. However, if you have noticed that often people do not understand what you say, or people have told you that your strong accent is difficult to follow, then you should try to work on your pronunciation before the exam.

You may sometimes not pronounce individual words correctly. This is expected and this will not affect your test result. It's very difficult to know how to say every word in a foreign language correctly, especially when you haven't heard or used them very often.

The examiner, or other test taker if there is one in the room, may ask you to repeat what you said if they don't understand. If this happens don't worry. Even native language speakers sometimes misunderstand each other and need things to be repeated.

During the interview, try to speak a little more slowly than you usually do and pronounce the words as clearly as you can. You are not expected to speak at a fast speed so it's better to slow down a bit and focus on speaking clearly and well.

To practise, try listening carefully to the way native speakers speak. Does the tone rise or fall in some sentences? Which words are pronounced or stressed more strongly? How are individual words pronounced? Listening to friends and family who speak English well will help you in your own pronunciation. Ask them to speak to you in English at all times so you can listen to their pronunciation and copy it. Watching movies, the news or any television programmes in English that you enjoy will help you to tune in to the way people speak English. You will then be able to copy that way when you speak.

You will be expected to understand 'standard' English'. This is a variety of English that many people think is better as it shows none of the regional or non-standard differences. This English is often used in the media and by public figures, such as news readers and politicians. As you will only be expected to understand standard English and that is spoken in a clear way, you probably won't find it useful to watch soap operas or films where people use street language, such as slang, or speak with very heavy regional accents. Accents found in these programmes do not provide a good model for you to copy when you want to work on your pronunciation.

Some people try recording themselves to see how they sound speaking English. Try to do this on your mobile. This is very good practice to help you understand how you actually sound when you speak English. You could then record someone who speaks English well, such as a friend, family member or even someone from the television, and then try to record yourself repeating the same words and sentences. Listen back to yourself. Did you say the words and sentences in the same way?

How well your speak

The examiner will be listening to how easy you find it to say what you want to say and to express yourself. You should be able to use sentences that are sometimes short and sometimes quite long but are not very complicated. It's better not to be too ambitious and try to use long sentences with complicated grammar that you are not confident about. Keep to sentences that you use often and just focus on trying to say them clearly with few grammar mistakes.

You should be able to keep going when you talk. The examiner will especially be looking at this when you have to give your short talk in the test. At times you can stop and pause, but you should be able to keep talking without much help from the examiner. If you find it difficult to remember what you wanted to say, you can't think of the words or how to say something, then leave that point and go on to the next thing you wanted to say. If you remember later, you can say *'Oh yes, before I wanted to say…'* Remember, the examiner is not judging the quality of the content of your talk, but just how well you can speak English. It doesn't matter if you forget words or what you wanted to say sometimes as long as you can continue to speak and do not come to a complete stop.

You may feel that you haven't expressed yourself well and something you said wasn't clear. If you feel this, then you could try to correct that by saying something like: *'What I meant is…'* or *'I mean to say…'*

If you can't think of a particular word you want to use and you come to a stop, then you could say *'Sorry, I forgot the word'* or *'I can't think of the word now'*. Native speakers do this all the time so it's perfectly normal to pause if you forget a word now and again, and the examiner won't think badly of you for it. You could think of a different word to use that has a similar meaning, explain what the word means or just move on to your next point. Try to continue speaking as best as you can and not let this affect you in the interview.

At times, you may need a few seconds to think what you want to say so you can say it well and correctly. Again, this is perfectly OK for B1 level. You are not expected to speak very quickly and without pausing now and again, so take your time and concentrate on speaking as well as you can.

Your accuracy

The examiner will not expect you to speak perfectly and without making any mistakes. However, the meaning of what you say should be quite clear and not cause the listener, who is the examiner or the other test taker if there is one with you, to have any problems understanding you. As we saw before, the subjects are ones that you often meet in your daily life such as the family, travel and transport so you should be able to talk quite confidently and be able to fully show the examiner how accurate your grammar is.

If you find that people do not always understand you when you speak in English, this may be because you are not using the language correctly. You can try to improve your grammar by doing some grammar exercises you can find in books or on the internet on particular grammar points that you find difficult. For example, in the interview you will be expected to show that you can use the past tense of some irregular verbs well. Do you feel confident about the past of *fly, drive* and *swim?* If you don't immediately think of *flew, drove* and *swam* then perhaps you can do some practice on this area.

Reading is a known way to improve grammatical accuracy. Try to read as much as you can before the test. You can read anything that you are interested in. If you don't have much time, then choose short articles from easy to read newspapers such as the free newspapers. As you read, try to pay attention to how the sentences are formed.

If you live with friends or family members or work with people who speak English well, ask them to correct you when they notice you make a mistake. Tell them that you have to take a test that is very important for you and would like their help with your English. Most people would like to help. However, it's often the case that many people who were born in the UK are not familiar with grammar or how to explain it, so you might find it more helpful to ask for help from people who have had to learn English like you.

If you think that your English level, or the level of the person you are helping is very weak, then a short intensive English course that focuses on reaching B1 level might be the answer. Using grammar well is often a major part of such courses.

How well you interact

In the interview you will be expected to interact with the examiner, or the other test taker if there is one. This means that you will need to listen carefully to what is being said and to respond well. The examiner will be checking to see how well you interact with them and the other test taker and react to what is being said.

Expect to be asked questions during your time in the interview room and be ready to answer as well as you can. The exam is not the time to day dream!

You will also be expected to ask questions too so be ready for this. You could for example ask the examiner or other test taker for opinions and information. You should do this as politely as you can. The exam is quite a formal situation so you will be expected to use language that is appropriate. This means that slang and language that is over familiar is best avoided.

Try not to be shy and to speak as much as you can in the interview. Do not wait for permission to ask a question or respond to something that has been said. If you are as active as you can in saying something and contributing to the discussion or conversation then this will give a good impression as it will show that you can communicate confidently.

Show how you feel about what has been said by responding with comments and expressions that do this. You could, for example, show surprise by saying 'Really?' Or you could show that you feel sad by saying 'That's a pity' or 'I'm sorry to hear that.'

When you feel that you want to react or respond to something someone said, then think about the language you can use to do this so you can make a suitable comment.

At all times you will need to show how well you can speak English and impress the examiner. For example, you could reply with one word, *'yes'*, to the question *'Do you agree with me?'* However, this would not be a very good answer. This is a correct and accurate answer, but it doesn't really show the examiner a good range of vocabulary and help the conversation to go on very much. A better answer would be a longer answer such as *'Yes, but I'm not sure I completely agree with you'*.

Your listening skills

The key to improving your listening skills in English is to do lots and lots of practice. Before we look at how you can do that let's remind ourselves of what listening skills you are expected to show in the B1 English test.

You are expected to understand and follow the key points of conversations and long discussions about familiar topics that are taking place around you. You are also expected to understand questions directed at you and to respond to them. If you are taking the IELTS Life Skills exam, then you will also have to listen to two different recordings and to answer some questions on what you have heard,

The examiner will not expect you to understand people who are speaking very fast or talking about something you know nothing about. You are expected just to follow people speaking slowly and clearly about everyday subjects. If you are doing the IELTS Life Skills test then you will also have to listen to some recordings. The people talking in the recordings will use Standard English and there will be no heavy regional accents for you to try and understand.

If you live in an English speaking country then you can go out and try to understand what people are saying around you. You could do this, for example, when you are waiting for a bus or looking round the shops. Notice what people say in different situations such as when the shop assistant gives them their change.

Ask your friends and family members who speak English well to talk to you only in English so you can practise listening to them. Perhaps you could even have a new rule that only English is spoken in your home until you have done your test!

Try to watch programmes or films where people speak clearly and don't use any strong accents. At first you may find it useful to use the subtitles in English as you can watch to see how the words are pronounced. English is not pronounced as it is written as it is in many other languages. This can be confusing as often people pronounce every letter they read as they do in their own language. For example, we do not pronounce the b in *debt* but pronounce this as *det*. You will become more aware of this if you read the subtitles while you watch. Over time, try to watch without looking at the subtitles to become more familiar with the sounds.

Make an effort to make time to watch programmes and films in English in your free time. People who only watch programmes in their own language often are not used to listening to English. As a result, their listening skills are not very strong and they do not do well in the exam.

You can do more practice by listening to recordings that you can find on some English language websites that are aimed at B1 students such as yourself.   The British Council website includes many helpful recordings and video clips about life in the UK and UK culture which is excellent practice at www.learnenglish. britishcouncil.org. The British Council also has a skills page with recordings especially for B1 learners who want to practise their listening skills at www.learnenglishteens.britishcouncil.org.

If you are taking the IELTS Life Skills test then look out for recordings with announcements such as at a train station and extracts of short radio news to help you prepare for the listening task.

Chapter 5

The Interview

Before the test day

After you receive your confirmation of your test date and time plan out your route to the test centre carefully. Look at how much time you will need to reach the centre. You will need to be at the test centre 30 minutes before your interview. It is very important that you are not late or else you will miss your time slot and may need to book, and pay for, another test. A good idea is to research the location of the test centre days before your interview. Check how long it will take you to get there and what's the easiest transport to use. Will you need a place to park your car if you take one? Find out about parking spaces nearby and how much you need to pay so you are fully prepared.

Make sure that you have all the correct documents such as your passport to take. Try to have them all ready before the day so you are not slowed down by searching for them in a panic in the morning.

On the day

You may well be feeling nervous and this is expected as it's probably a very important exam for you. However, many test takers have said that they had very good experiences and there was no reason to feel nervous. Many people who took the test said that the people in the centres treated them very well. And the more you know about the exam and the more prepared you are will mean the better the experience will be for you!

Remember, you will only be allowed entry to the test centre 30 minutes before your interview time. Don't risk being late as you may have to reschedule. Make sure you are there in very good time and ready to enter when you are told.

Hopefully your interview will run on time. However, be ready for any delays and allow for this. You may, for example, have to tell a family member before you go in that they may need to be patient if they are waiting for you outside.

The exam will be held in very secure conditions and you will probably have limited access to your mobile. This is quite normal and nothing to worry about. However, do be ready for security checks such as the checking of your documents.

During the Interview

You need to reach a certain level of English language ability to be given a pass grade and will need to show this to the examiner. During the spoken test the examiners will be listening carefully to assess your language and listening skills. They will want to see if your English skills match the language requirements of B1. If you try to relax and be ready to interact with the examiner and the other person in the room, then you will more likely be able to show the examiner what you can do in English.

As we saw before, it's important to try to talk as much as you can and answer the questions as fully as you can. The examiner will then be able to judge your English level well.

During the test the examiner will probably look at a checklist to see how closely your English level matches. The examiner may have this list on the desk in front of them and look at it during the test. However, you do not need to worry about what the examiner is doing during the test, but just need to focus on speaking as well as you can.

Chapter 6

Language practice

The examiner will be looking to see that you can use language at an elementary level or B1 level. In this section you will find examples of language at this level that will give you an idea of the difficulty of the language. You will see that the language level that has been set for this test is not particularly complicated. The language you will be expected to produce is at the level that will enable you to function in society.

Below you will find some examples of the language you will hear and can use in the exam. There are examples of the questions that you may be asked and that you could ask to the examiner or other test taker. There are also some examples of sentences to show that you can use practical English that meet the language requirements the examiner will be looking for.

What are the questions like?

Below you will find some typical questions at this level, the B1 level, the examiner or the other test taker may ask you. These questions are intended to help you to judge your skills in answering them, and give you an idea of the level of difficulty of the questions in the exam.

As well as the examiner asking you questions in the interview you will also have to ask the examiner, or the other test taker if there is one, questions too. This will be expected of you so you must make the effort to do this. These questions will help you prepare to do this.

Do not prepare for your exam by memorising these questions as they will not be identical to the questions you will be asked in the exam.

Questions that cover the language requirements

Questions on the **past**

- When did you arrive in this country?
- When were you born?
- Where did you used to live when you were a child?
- What did you do yesterday?
- What were your hobbies when you were a child?
- What did you do with your family last weekend?

Questions on **recent events and experiences**

- How long have you lived here?
- Have you visited any interesting places recently?
- Have you done anything interesting recently?
- Where have you been since you arrived in the UK?
- What cities or towns have you visited here?

Questions on **likes/dislikes and preferences**

- How do you prefer to travel – by bus, train or car? Why?
- What do you enjoy doing in your free time?
- Is there anything about (your job/town) you dislike?
- How do you prefer to spend your evenings?
- What type of films are you keen on?
- What type of music do you usually listen to?
- Are you interested in watching the news?

Questions to ask for **reasons**

- What is the reason for that?
- Why do you think that?
- Is that because…..?
- Is there a reason for that in your view?
- What is the cause of that?
- Is that because…?
- What do you think is the reason behind that?

Questions to ask for **opinions and feelings**

- What is your opinion?
- What do you think about this?
- What is your view?
- And you? What do you think?
- How do you feel about this?
- What's your feeling?
- Do you have a different opinion?

Questions to ask for **explanations**

- Can you explain this to me?
- What do you mean?
- What do you mean by that?
- What is the meaning of that?
- Can you give me an explanation?

Questions to **check meaning:**

- Do you mean...?
- What do you mean exactly?
- Can you explain what you mean?
- Could you say it again in a different way?
- Are you saying ...?

Questions to ask for **agreement**

- Do you agree with me?
- Are we in agreement?
- Do you go along with that?
- Is that alright with you?
- Do you think so too?

Questions **on future plans and predictions**

- Where are you planning to go for your next holiday?
- Who will win the next World Cup in your opinion?
- What are you going to do next weekend?
- What are your plans for this summer?
- When will you next visit your family back home?
- When do you think we will all use electric cars?
- Who do you think might be the next US President?

Questions on **future possibility and certainty**

- Do you think you might....?

- How likely is it that …?

- Will you possibly…?

- How much chance is there of that?

- How sure are you about that?

- Are you certain that will happen?

- Is that a certainty?

- Don't you think that's impossible?

- Do you think that might happen?

- Is that a real possibility?

Questions on subjects

You will have to talk about everyday subjects that you are very familiar with. These subjects include your family, transport, your home, work or college, your health, your hobbies, shopping, free time and entertainment, education/training, transport and travel, housing, and events and experiences in the past. Below are some typical examples of the questions that use the language up to B1 level. The questions below will give you an idea of the type of questions you will be asked during the interview

Remember, answering the questions well and as fully as you can will give the examiner a good picture of your English language level.

Questions on **your family and friends**

- How long have you been married?

- How many people are there in your family?

- How do you and your family celebrate special occasions?

- Have you been on holiday recently with your family?

- What do you enjoy doing at the weekends with your family?
- How long have you known your best friend?
- Where and when did you meet your best friend?
- How important is it to have many friends?
- What's the reason people have friends?
- Are you planning to see your best friend in the near future?

Questions on **your workplace or college**

- What kind of work or studies are you currently doing?
- How long have you been doing this work or studies?
- How much time do you typically spend at college/work?
- What do you enjoy most about your work or studies?
- How many people do you work with?
- How well do you get on with the people you work with?
- Why did you decide to take your present job?
- Is there anything you dislike about your job or your college course?
- Have you made many friends since you've worked/studied there?
- Do you think you'll change your job in the near future?

Questions on **health**

- Do you think you are a healthy person?
- What healthy activities did you used to do when you were a child?
- What do you prefer to do, diet or exercise?

- Why don't people do more exercise?
- How can we persuade people to eat more healthy food?
- Have you ever been on a diet?
- What's more important: health, family or money?
- Have you ever stayed in a hospital?
- What's your opinion on the health service here?
- Are planning to do any healthy activities at the weekend?

Questions on **festivals**

- Have you ever been to a festival?
- What festivals are celebrated in your country?
- Why is it important to celebrate festivals?
- How long does the festival last?
- Would you prefer to celebrate at home or at an outdoor event?
- What's the best thing about this festival for you?
- What did you do on the day of the festival?
- Have the way people celebrate this festival changed in the last 20 years?
- How important is food/dancing to this festival?
- What festival will you celebrate next?

Questions on **transport**

- Have you ever missed a train or a plane?
- What transport do you prefer to use on a daily basis?
- How can we persuade more people to use public transport?

- How long did your journey here take today?
- Have you ever fallen off a bicycle, motorbike or a horse?
- What transport did your parents use when you were a child?
- Why do many people use their cars instead of public transport?
- What the difference between taking the bus or train in your experience?
- How much time do you spend on public transport each day?
- Will public transport get better or worse in the future? Why?

Questions on **travel**

- Have you travelled anywhere recently?
- Have you done much travelling in this country?
- Who do you prefer to travel with and why?
- What do you think is the best way to travel – by car or by plane?
- How much time do you spend travelling in a week?
- Do you enjoy travelling? Why?
- Which countries would you like to visit and why?
- Would you rather stay at home in the summer or visit another city?
- Have you planned to go anywhere in the next few months?
- What's the most beautiful place you've ever visited?

Questions on **your home**

- What does your home look like from the outside?
- Who currently lives with you at home?

- How long have you lived in your home?
- In what way is your home today different from your home when you were a child?
- How much time do you spend at home?
- Have you met your neighbours?
- What changes would you like to make to your home?
- Do you think you will you stay in your current house in the near future?
- Which do you prefer, a home with a garden or a home without a garden?
- Have you made any changes to your home since you moved in?

Questions on **recent experiences**

- What has been an interesting experience for you recently?
- Have you been on any days out recently?
- Have you been successful in anything recently?
- Have you ever visited the seaside in the UK?
- What happened on a recent trip you had?
- Has anything new happened to you in recent weeks?
- Have you tried to do anything in a different way recently?
- Have you seen anything that made you laugh recently?
- What celebrations have you had with your family lately?
- What has been your experience of using the public transport system here?

Questions on **hobbies**

- How many hobbies do you have?
- Have you had the same hobbies since you were a child?
- What's the reason people spend time on hobbies?
- How much time do you spend on your hobbies?
- Do your family members have any hobbies?
- Will you continue with this hobby in the future?
- What hobbies did you used to have when you were a child?
- Do you think only rich people can have time for hobbies?
- Can you explain what this hobby involves?
- When did you start this hobby?

Questions on **shopping and buying things**

- What kind of shops do you prefer?
- How often do you go shopping?
- Have you bought anything expensive recently?
- Have you ever been to the January sales?
- How much time do you spend shopping in a week?
- What's important for you when you go shopping?
- How long do you usually spend in the supermarket?
- Why do you think people spend more money than they have?
- Which supermarkets are the best in your opinion?
- Are you planning to buy anything in the near future?

Questions on **education/training**

- How many students were in your school?
- Did you enjoy school? Why/Why not?
- Why do people think education is so important?
- Who was your favourite teacher and why?
- Do you think it's better to go to university or straight to a job?
- How much homework did you do when you were at school?
- Have you received much training to do your job?
- What training course would you like to do next?
- How many times have you visited your children's school?
- Do you think you might do some further studies?

Questions on **your job and work in general**

- How long have you been in your job?
- What was your first job?
- What's the best way to find a job?
- What do you like most about your job?
- How many people do you work with?
- How much time do you spend at work each week?
- Have you ever worked at weekends or during public holidays?
- What job did you want to do when you were a child?
- Would you prefer a boring but well paid job or an interesting but low paid one?
- What job would you like to do?

Questions on **free time/entertainment**

- How do you prefer to spend your free time?
- What do you and your family do for entertainment in the evenings?
- Have you been to the cinema recently?
- How much time do you spend on the internet?
- Have you ever watched a film in 3D?
- What do people back in your country usually do in their free time?
- When was the last time you went to the cinema?
- Do you have any plans to go to the theatre or cinema?
- What entertainment do you enjoy the most?
- What did you used to do in your free time when you were a child?

How to give good answers in the interview

The examiner will ask you questions throughout the exam and if you are with another test taker then you will have to answer questions from them too. So what is a very good answer? A good answer is one which shows your ability to speak at B1 level and this means that you should answer the question accurately, be easy to understand, and make no or few grammatical mistakes. As much as possible you will need to show that you can use a good range of relevant words when you answer the question too.

Of course it's better if you can say as much as you when you make your answer. The examiner cannot judge your English level well if you just reply with one or two word answers. For example you will not give a very good impression if you just reply *with 'Yes'* to the question *'Is it easy to travel around the place you live?'* Instead, an answer such as *'Yes, I think it is. I've never had any problems'* will have a much more positive effect on the examiner as this will show that you can respond well and can use language at the B1 level. An even better answer is a longer answer such as

'Yes, I think it is. I've never had any problems. But compared to a capital city like London there aren't many choices of transport. We can only use buses and taxis.'

You can find some practice on answering the test questions later in the book.

Using practical language

The examiner will want to know that you can do certain things in English such as *make suggestions, persuade someone to do something* and *ask for information* and these are listed in the guidelines for the English language level B1. The more language you use to do this in the exam, the more fully you will meet the requirements. Remember, the exam is an opportunity for you to show how much English you know. The examiner will be listening all the time to everything you say. So take the chance to include as much of this language in your conversation naturally and as much as you can.

Below are some of the functions that the examiner will be looking for together with some language expressions you can use:

Make suggestions

- How about…?
- I suggest we do this…
- Why don't we go/do…?

- Shall we…?
- Would it be a good idea to..?
- Have you thought about …ing?

Ask for information

- I'd like to know…
- Can you let me know…?
- Could you please tell me ….
- Could you give me some information about …
- Would you tell me …
- I'd like to have some information about …

Persuade someone

- I think it's the best thing to do
- Don't you think it's a good idea?
- I'm sure the result will be better
- Come on. It will be interesting!
- I'm sure it will be great/fun/interesting/useful.
- You'll be happy you made this decision!
- This will definitely help
- We might have a problem if we don't do this

Give your opinion

- In my view …
- I feel/think that…

- In my opinion…
- If you ask me…I think…
- As I see it…
- Personally, I think…

Say you don't understand

- I'm not sure I know what you mean
- I don't follow you
- I don't see what you mean
- I'm not sure I got your point
- I don't understand what you are saying
- Sorry, I didn't get your point

Say you didn't hear something

- Could you repeat that please?
- Sorry, I didn't catch that
- I'm afraid I missed that
- Could you say that again?
- Sorry, what did you say?

Agree with someone

- I agree with you
- I completely agree (strong)
- I couldn't agree with you more (strong)
- That's not true
- You're absolutely right (strong)

- That's how I feel

Disagree with someone

- I don't think so
- I don't agree
- I'm afraid I disagree
- I totally disagree (strong)
- I don't think that's true
- No, I'm not sure about that

Interrupt someone

- Could I interrupt and say …
- Can I say something?
- Can I add something here?
- Is it okay if I jump in here?
- Sorry to interrupt, but...

Compare and contrast

- In comparison, I'd say...
- This one is stronger/bigger/taller etc. than that.
- X isn't as big/tall as x
- It's more interesting that the others
- It's worse/better than …
- To compare, x is bigger than x
- It's similar in that….
- In contrast, this one is….

- However, this one is...
- On the other hand...

State a purpose

- The aim is to…
- My goal is to …
- We need to do this **so that** …
- We need to do this **in order to** …
- The main purpose of this is to…
- **For that reason,** we should…

Talk about future possibilities and certainty

- That might happen
- It's possible that this will …
- It's very possible that will happen
- It's likely to happen…
- I'm sure that people will …
- I'm positive that I'll…
- People think it's certain that …

Talk about duration of events

- The match will last 90 minutes
- It takes two hours to reach
- It will go on for at least an hour
- It will continue for a few hours
- The games will take place over a few weeks.

Practice test questions and answers

Look at the questions below. Choose the best answer. You can find the answers at the end of this section.

1. *How long have you been at college?*

a. It takes about 30 minutes by bus but my father usually drives me

b. I've been here three months.

c. Three months now.

d. Well, I started in September so I've been there for three months now.

2. *What did you used do in your free time when you were a child?*

a. I used to play football with my brothers in the local park. I was always the goal-keeper!

b. I didn't have any free time.

c. I played with my friends.

d. I can't remember.

3. *What's the reason people have friends?*

a. What do you think?

b. To do things with, I guess.

c. To help you when you have problems. Especially when your family is far away.

d. I have quite a lot. At work everyone is very friendly and we spend time together at weekends.

4. *How much time do you spend shopping?*

a. Every Saturday morning with my wife. We usually take the car as it's easier.

b. I don't like shopping. It's boring.

c. About one hour.

d. Not a lot. I usually just go with my wife on Saturday mornings. Although I don't enjoy it very much.

5. *What did you see the last time you went to the cinema?*

a. I love watching comedy films.

b. Sorry, I can't remember.

c. I'm a big fan of action movies so it was the latest James Bond film.

d. Spectre.

6. *Have you ever been to a festival?*

a. Sorry, I don't understand

b. Yes, I have. I went to a fantastic rock festival near my home last year.

c. No, I don't like crowds.

d. Yes, once or twice.

7. *What do you think is the best way to stay healthy?*

a. Anything but smoking. It is the worst.

b. Personally, I feel people need to be more active and take more exercise.

c. I am very healthy. I enjoy walking and playing with my children in the garden.

d. Make sure you eat good food.

8. *Are you interested in watching the news?*

a. What do you mean?

b. Yes, I like the news.

c. Yes, I am. I feel it's important to follow the news every day to see what's happening in the world.

d. Yes. I do. I watch it at 10 o'clock every evening after dinner.

9. *How much free time do you have?*

a. Not much. I've worked overtime a lot recently and been very busy.

b. I have no free time.

c. I go to the cinema often with my kids and we laugh a lot.

d. Not a lot. How about you?

10. *Who was your favourite teacher when you were at school and why?*

a. His name was Peter, and he was my maths teacher.

b. I used to love lessons with my maths teacher, Peter. He was very patient with us.

c. My maths teacher, Peter. He was strict but fair.

d. I didn't like any of them.

11. *Would you rather stay at home in the summer or visit another city?*

a. I'm fascinated by history so I'd rather visit a city and preferably an old one.

b. At home.

c. I don't like to travel.

d. I'm very busy and I have got three children. Home is good for me and my family.

12. *Do you think you will stay in your present house or move?*

a. We will stay in this house. We do a lot of work – painting, in the garden, you know.

b. Yes, move.

c. I'll probably stay in my current house for now. I have no plans to move.

d. No, I don't like my house much.

13. *What are the advantages of travelling by bus?*

a. I don't understand.

b. No, I never travel by bus, I prefer to use my car.

c. Sorry, could you say that again?

d. Travelling by bus is great. I really like it.

14. *What hobby would you like to try?*

a. I like painting and reading novels.

b. I don't have any hobbies.

c. I don't have enough time to try new hobbies.

d. I'd like to try drawing. I was quite good when I was at school.

15. *What's your house like?*

a. I don't understand.

b. Sorry, do you want me to describe my house?

c. I like my house. It's better than my first house.

d. Two bedrooms, one living room, one kitchen and no garden.

16. *What places have you visited recently?*

a. I've been to Manchester and Brighton recently to visit my friends living there.

b. Manchester and Brighton

c. Please can you repeat the question?

d. I drove to Manchester last week to visit my friends living there.

17. *What will you buy next in the shops?*

a. Bread and potatoes

b. I'll go to the shops later today to buy food for dinner.

c. Many things – a mobile, clothes, food, things for the house. Usual.

d. I'll buy a new mobile. Mine isn't working because it fell into some water.

18. *How often do you celebrate special occasions?*

a. Very often. I enjoy getting together with friends and family and chatting about news.

b. One time a month.

c. What do you mean by special occasions?

d. Rarely. It's good to see friends and family and I like it very much.

19. *In what way are schools different here to schools in your country?*

a. Same really. No difference,

b. I like the schools here. The teachers in my country are very hard.

c. I think the subjects the children study here are very different compared to in my country.

d. My son likes the school very much.

20. *What are you going to do this weekend with your children?*

a. Go to the park with my son.

b. I usually take my son to the park.

c. Well, it's my son's birthday on Saturday so we're planning to go the park in the morning. Then we'll go to his favourite restaurant.

d. We'll go to the park and then visit my son's favourite restaurant. After that we'll have a very big lunch.

Answers:

1 d 2 a 3 c 4 d 5 c 6 b 7 b 8 c 9 a 10 b 11 a 12 c 13 c 14 d 15 b 16 a 17 d 18 a 19 c 20 c

Important

The best responses answer the question that was asked exactly, answer the question with complete sentences and show a good range of words and grammar.

The answers above are the best answers for these questions. However, you will do better if you try to extend your answers as much as you can and give full answers in two or three sentences.

Hot tips

20 General Tips for the B1 test

1. Speak as clearly as you can

2. Don't speak too fast

3. Take a little time to answer the questions

4. Answer questions as fully as you can

5. Add more information to extend your answers.

6. Don't be afraid to ask the examiner or other person to repeat.

7. Check you understood correctly if you are unsure.

8. Don't try to memorise large pieces of information

9. Speak as naturally as you can

10. Make an effort to show your English language skills to their maximum

11. Use words and phrases you are comfortable with

12. Avoid language that is very informal or slang words

13. Use a variety of words and don't just repeat the same ones

14. Use a word with a similar meaning if you can't remember the right word

15. Try to keep talking with only short pauses.

16. Plan out your route and the time needed to get to the centre.

17. Arrive at the centre early.

18. Take the centre phone number in case of a problem on the way

19. Check you have the right documents to take.

20. Practice with the questions in the language practice section.

10 More Tips for the IELTS B1 Life Skills Test

1. Prepare by listening to the audio recordings on the IELTS Skills Test website

2. Greet the other test taker and be friendly to them

3. Ask the other test taker to repeat if you don't understand

4. Make use of the full minute to write notes and prepare your talk

5. Use notes or words in a mind map and not full sentences when preparing for your talk.

6. Make comments on what the other test taker says

7. Listen to the other test taker's talk carefully so you can ask questions

8. Ask the examiner to repeat or to explain the instructions if you don't understand

9. Be ready to talk to the other test taker to make a decision together

10. Take notes or make a mind map when listening to the recordings

10 More Tips for the Trinity GESE Grade 5 test

1. Prepare your topic form well in advance

2. Include enough material so your talk lasts no longer than 5 minutes

3. Check you have included the language of B1 as found in the Language Practice

4. Practice your talk and get friends or family members to ask you questions

5. Prepare some questions to ask the examiner about your topic

6. Check you can talk about the subjects given in the conversation part

7. Work on your vocabulary for the subjects such as transport in the Trinity conversation

8. Watch videos of the B1 exam on the Trinity SELT website for the Grade 5 test

9. Ask the examiner at least one question during the conversation

10. Read and do the exercises on the Trinity SELT website for the Grade 5 test

A few final words

Much of the information and advice you have found in this book has been to help you to prepare for the English language test and to pass it. However, you will also find that following all this advice will, and perhaps more importantly, help you to get by and communicate more easily in English with people you meet every day such as when you are at work, at the doctor's or in a shop.

The skills that the English language exam tests such as making questions, interacting with others, and listening are all skills that we need to participate in life around us, in our communities and in society at large. Learning to speak English well will help you to feel more confident, comfortable and able to deal with the different situations you will typically meet.

We wish you the very best both in the test and in your future in your new permanent home, the UK.

Here are some final tips to help motivate you to practise your English before the test.

- Ask a person you have just met lots of questions. People like it when you show you are interested in them and this is a good way to make friends.

- Have some fun and practise listening to people answer your questions to see if you think they would pass the B1 test. Are their answers full and accurate enough to pass? Is their vocabulary very simple or do they show a good range?

- Ask friends and family to repeat and speak more slowly if you don't understand them the first time. Try to understand why exactly you didn't understand when they spoke.

- If someone doesn't understand you when you speak, ask them to tell you why. Was it your pronunciation of a word or did you use the wrong word in the first place perhaps?

- Build up your confidence by asking simple questions at first to people such as *'Where do you live?'* When you feel more confident then go on to ask more difficult questions such as *'Where would you prefer to live, in a city or the countryside?'*

- When someone asks you a question, answer and then ask them a question back. Think of it as a game where you need to find out some information about everyone who asks you a question.

- Ask for feedback from friends and family on your progress. Have they noticed your English has improved?

- Plan where you will go to celebrate with your friends and family after you pass your test.

Sources used and some helpful websites

For practice in listening, grammar and vocabulary at B1 level go to www.examenglish.com/B1/index.php

For recordings and video clips about life in the UK and UK culture go to www.learnenglish.britishcouncil.org.

For listening practice especially for B1 learners go to www. learnenglishteens.britishcouncil.org.

Find short easy reading books to help you with your grammar and vocabulary at www.cambridge.org/gb/cambridgeenglish/catalog/ skills/cambridge-english-readers

For help with your tenses go to Cambridge English TV's website to watch the videos

For information and tips about the exam you are taking look at the Colleges' websites

For more information about Trinity College's GESE Grade 5 test go to www.**trinity**college.com/**SELT**

For more information about the IELTS Life Skills site go to www. ielts.org/test_takers_information/ielts_in_the_uk.aspx

You can find out more information about the English test at www. gov.uk/english-language/overview

To find more information about the Life in the UK test visit the home office website www.gov.uk/life-in-the-uk-test

For information about the CEFR - http://www.coe.int/t/dg4/ education/

Printed in Great Britain
by Amazon

17381191R00051